Barbie Doll
Exclusively for Timeless Creations
IDENTIFICATION & VALUES
BOOK III
By Margo Rana

Published by Hobby House Press, Inc.
Grantsville, Maryland 21536

The likeness of the Barbie doll and character, the color "Barbie pink" and other trademarks designated by ® and ™ are U.S. trademarks of Mattel, Inc., and are used under license. ©1996 Mattel, Inc. All Rights Reserved. Mattel makes no representation as to the authenticity of the materials contained herein. All opinions are those of the author and not of Mattel.

Bob Mackie® is a registered trademark.

Barbie® Doll Exclusively for Timeless Creations is an independent study by the author Margo Rana and published by Hobby House Press, Inc. The research and publication of this book were not sponsored in any way by the manufacturers of the dolls, the doll costumes, and the doll accessories featured in this study. Photographs of the collectibles were from dolls, costumes, or accessories belonging to Margo Rana at the time the picture was taken unless otherwise credited with the caption.

The information as to the ownership pertains to documentary materials contemporary with the doll or doll's accessories. Ownership of the registered trademark, the trademark, or the copyright may have expired or been transferred to another owner.

In order to capture the greatest detail of the dolls and accessories in the photographic process, the dolls and accessories will appear a different size than in real life.

The values given within this book are intended as value guides rather than arbitrarily set prices. The values quoted are as accurate as possible but in the case of errors, typographical, clerical, or otherwise, the author and publisher assume no liability nor responsibility for any loss incurred by users of this book.

Front Cover: (Top) Portrait in Taffeta, 1996. For more information see page 145. *(Bottom) Neptune Goddess,* 1992. For more information see page 31.
Title Page: Oshogatsu #1, 1995. For more information see page 132.
Table of Contents: Timeless Creations Catalogs. 1991 to 1996.
Back Cover: Pink Splendor, 1996. For more information see page 160.

ABOUT THE AUTHOR

Margo is lucky to live in Santa Barbara, California with her husband, three cats and a dog. Margo has been collecting Barbie dolls for over two decades, if you count her childhood days. She buys, sells and collects new, vintage and other 11-1/2" fashion and celebrity dolls. Margo started her business (Margo's) the same year that the Timeless Creations division was established. You could say they grew together.

If you were to ask Margo on a Monday which is her favorite doll, she would think long and hard and respond. If you ask her the same question on a Friday, she will have a different response. There are just too many wonderful dolls to be definitive. If the truth be known; it's her #2 brunette that has her heart because it was the first Barbie doll she ever owned and cherished.

Additional copies of this book may be purchased at $24.95 (plus postage and handling) from
Hobby House Press, Inc.
1 Corporate Drive
Grantsville, Maryland 21536
1-800-554-1447
or from
Margo's, 2726 De La Vina Street, Santa Barbara, CA 93105 • (805) 687-5677 • 24-hour Fax: (805) 569-0088
or from your favorite bookstore or dealer.

ISBN: 0-87588-474-1

TABLE OF CONTENTS

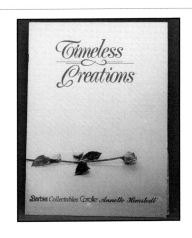

I have gotten tons of letters, cards, and calls of appreciation. Many of you wrote and encouraged me to write another book. There was a moment when I wasn't going to do any more, but there were so many positive and encouraging words about my work, that I decided to go forward with *Book III*.

The Timeless Creations Division of Mattel was the name assigned to the sales department developed to handle the sales of specialty Barbie dolls. This department, in conjunction with the specialty design division, would work hand-in-hand in nurturing Barbie® doll collectors. These collectors wanted limited editions, but also something more elaborate in regard to design, construction, and higher quality fabrics, and at the same time were willing to pay more to get it. The design department would create the dolls and the Timeless Creations Division would sell them.

Quite a few long-time employees were transferred from their departments into the specialty division. Utilizing an already established knowledgeable staff in the new specialty division would give the department the adrenaline it needed to get rolling. The specialty doll shops would relay information about what the collectors wanted.

It didn't take long at all for the "old timers" in the sales department, like Shirley Mallory, to report the public's desires to Mattel's design department. Then it was up to the design department to see to it that the design staff created the dolls and fashions that would send collectors into a buying frenzy. Before too long, selling was not a skill, but rather a paper chase. The orders flooded in the minute specialty stores all across the nation received their photos and catalogs. The sales division was constantly upgrading their computers to accommodate the influx of orders and to help maintain better control. Things would never be the same again! Not for the design department, not for the sales department, not for specialty stores, and especially not for the collector.

The new Timeless Creations sales division was an overnight success for Mattel. This, combined with the release of the 1988 Happy Holidays® Barbie doll, sent Mattel swirling. The design department would have to work fast and furiously to come up with fresh ideas and stimulate further sales. Within a few short years we would see not only porcelain Barbie dolls, but a new line of Barbie dolls created by the world-famous American designer, Bob Mackie.

The Gold Bob Mackie! She would become one of the most sought after dolls for years to come. Collectors who were in the habit of buying regular line Barbie dolls at the toy store for $4.99 were shocked to walk into a specialty doll shop and see a Barbie doll for $120. The doll was special, the shop was special, and many collectors wanted to feel that way about themselves. Suddenly a Gold Bob Mackie Barbie doll could make them feel special too.

Things would change again. Just a few years ago, Mattel took the Timeless Creations name that had been long and well established by the sales division and shared it with their own mail order division. This made it very confusing for collectors. Why were the wholesale and retail division sharing a name? Then, there was a far greater problem for the specialty stores. The mail order division had difficulties filling orders correctly. Once they even sent me someone else's dolls. I often wonder if the other collector ever got her order.

The Timeless Creations mail order division whose fullfilment center had been in Chatsworth, California has since closed. Mattel renamed the mail order division Barbie Collectibles and changed the center's location. They now put out several catalogs. Things seem to be going a lot smoother. Effective in mid-1996 the Timeless Creations Sales division was renamed Inside Sales, and the mail order division is now referred to as Barbie Collectibles.

When Mattel decided to direct market at the retail level, the market changed. The once limited edition dolls that collectors had placed on pedestals in their collections, were flooding the market. The specialty stores were no longer supplying the Barbie doll volume that they once had to the consumer. What many may not realize is that the specialty shop owners are often the Barbie doll experts who can answer the collecting questions: "How much is my doll worth?" "Do you buy retired dolls?" "I found this doll at a yard sale, who is she?" Collectors need to remember the important role that specialty shops hold in the Barbie doll market.

Don't be confused. Despite what I have said here, Barbie doll is nonetheless wonderful. The situation is merely changing. The doll is still sacred.

Just a few words about the value guide. It is just that, a guide. The Barbie doll market is volatile and changes frequently. By the time *Barbie Exclusives Book 1* was released, the market had changed radically. The primary reason is supply and demand. You can have a small supply and no demand which will keep prices low. If there is a small supply and big demand, this will cause higher prices. Some dolls are more likely to be found in certain parts of the country and not in others; therefore prices can vary from one part of the country to another. This can be tricky for the investor. For the collector, it is common knowledge that you should buy what you like. This way you will never be unhappy.

I was extremely pleased at so many glowing book reviews on *Barbie Exclusives Book I* and *Book II*. One of the most interesting ones I read indicated that I had blown it because I had taken my dolls out of their boxes, hence, devaluating them. I am first and foremost a collector. I buy, sell, trade, and collect. As a collector, taking my dolls out of their boxes and even throwing Barbie doll's card board carriers out, does not bother me in the least. For me, the fun is playing with the dolls, dressing and redressing them, making displays and participating in show-and-tells. Investment in my private collecting has never been the priority. Having fun with my dolls was and is my main interest. Each of you must decide for yourselves what makes you happy and just go with it. Whatever you decide I wish you as much pleasure as I have had in the past and hope to in the future.

I would also like to take a moment to thank those who assisted in sharing to make this book particularly special to me. Shirley Mallory, for seeing to it that I could get the dolls in time to meet the deadline for this book and for sharing information and photos, and just plain being there for me; Bob Gardner for sharing information, facts, and dolls, for proofing my manuscripts to insure what I was writing was accurate; Joan Mitchell for correcting my mis-spells, typos, and grammar; Ruby Knauss, for getting all the designers in her department to bring their favorite doll for an early morning photo-shoot, so that I could share this with you; Judy Schizas for arranging to have all the designers list their dolls; and to the designers whose ideas are endless and keep Barbie doll collectors so very happy.

Sincerely,

Margo Rana

Margo Rana

MATTEL DESIGNERS

I thought you might like to see some of the Mattel design staff who are responsible for creating some of the dolls you see in this book. I had requested that each of the designers bring their favorite Barbie doll that they designed. This photo was taken at the Mattel design center especially for *Exclusively Timeless Book III*. It is unfortunate that I was not able to have all of the designers together for this photo. I tried. Some times things don't always go the way they should. I hope that this is not true in your search for your favorite Barbie dolls.

Top Row: Ann Driskill; Ruby Knauss — Director, Barbie Collector Dolls & Collectibles; Janet Goldblatt — *Snow Princess* Barbie Doll; Abbe Littleton — Barbie Doll as *Glinda the Good Witch* (Wizard of Oz); Nora Harri-Trezona — Barbie doll as *Little Bo Peep*. ***Bottom Row:*** Robert Best — *My Fair Lady Ascot* Barbie Doll; Carol Spencer — *Golden Jubilee* Barbie Doll; Sharon Zuckerman — *My Fair Lady*, Ken Doll as *Professor Henry Higgins*; Damaris Vidal — *My Fair Lady Ballgown* Barbie Doll. *Photo by Mattel.*

Celebrate Mardi Gras with Barbie

Banners, balls, costumes and floats! It's Mardi Gras time in New Orleans. And Barbie is dressed for the occasion. For over 100 years, Rex, the king of Mardi Gras, and his magnificent floats have paraded through the streets of the Vieux Carré. Women watch from old ironwork balconies, while children in the crowds below scramble for trinkets thrown from the floats. Later at the grand balls, masked women and men in glittering costumes dance the night away!

Mardi Gras
#4930 • 1987 • $125

Mardi Gras Barbie doll was to have been the start of a series called the American Beauties Collection. For some unknown reason the series was dropped after only two dolls. Barbie doll celebrates Mardi Gras in New Orleans in an unusual orchid colored ball gown that instantly changes into a parade dress.
Designed by: Carol Spencer

Army
#3966 • 1989 • $55

Army Barbie doll would be the second and the last in the collection known as American Beauties. The very next year Mattel shifted their thoughts and began a new series called Stars 'n Stripes. Most collectors regard this first Army doll as part of Stars 'n Stripes. I tend to do that too. Technically this is a gift set. It comes with an extra uniform for day wear. Barbie doll's long skirt is the official regulation officer's evening uniform for formal dinners, embassy parties, and any other formal military functions. The doll you see featured here belongs to my friend Carolyn. Hers is a lot nicer than mine. I tried to get her to let me keep hers, but it didn't work out.

Military galas are grand!

Barbie is dressed with elegance in an authentic Army officer's evening uniform. She wears regulation form-fitting jacket with gold braid, dress shoulder knots and military decorations, a long graceful skirt, and even regulation "pearl" earrings and ring. Pretty and proud. Barbie attends official military dinners, embassy parties, and many other formal affairs around the world with the men and women who serve their country.

Contents: Doll, short formal jacket, long skirt, short skirt, blouse, hat, pretend pearl jewelry, pumps.

9

Colonial

#12578 • 1994 • $30

I love this collection! In my opinion the American Stories Series is the best value Mattel currently offers. Each and every doll in the grouping has lots to offer, including accessories, excellent workmanship, good quality fabrics, and a bit of American history. The fashions have been well researched and presented on the most successful doll of all time. Each comes with a little storybook that gives Barbie doll a story-line-life of her own. Could Mattel have created this category in direct competition with the American Girl Collection by The Pleasant Company? If so, then let's see the high quality wood furniture and accessories that should go with these girls!

Designed by: Sharon Zuckerman

Pilgrim
#12577 • 1994 • $30

New Englanders in particular choose this wonderful doll to help decorate at Thanksgiving. The only thing missing is a turkey. This doll was to have come to the Americas on the Mayflower. Notice that four out of the six dolls to date have aprons on, and all of them wear a hat or, in the case of the American Indian, a headpiece, a tradition long lost in daily attire.

Designed by: Sharon Zuckerman

Pioneer
#12680 • 1994 • $30

Fancying myself as an amateur clothing historian, I must say that Sharon Zuckerman really captured fashion history with each and every one of these dolls. The first Pioneer doll for Mattel is fabulous. I love the way they painted her two-tone eyes to coordinate with her "go-to-town and sell the apples" dress. Barbie doll might have traded those apples for eggs at the local mercantile store.

Designed by: Sharon Zuckerman

Pioneer II
#14756 • 1995 • $30

Some collectors were disturbed that Mattel would have two Pioneers in the series, but for those of us who take them out of the boxes, we can really do a nice story-telling display when the dolls are all related. After milking the cow Barbie doll can offer needy strangers some nutrition. She is quite the good neighbor.

Designed by: Sharon Zuckerman

13

Civil War Nurse
#14612 • 1995 • $40

To date, Civil War Nurse Barbie doll has been the best selling in the collection. The doll ties in well with the Scarlett O'Hara Series. This period piece is sought after by Civil War collectors as well as by anyone in the medical field. There are those who want to have her with their Dr. Barbie dolls and Nurse Whitney doll.

Designed by: Sharon Zuckerman

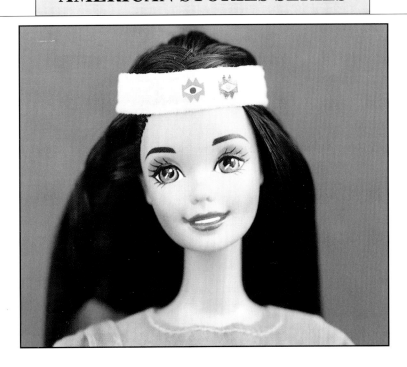

American Indian
#14715 • 1995 • $30

Barbie doll holds her cousin Baby Blue Feather. Her dress matches his bundling. The first time Mattel used the mold for Baby Blue Feather was in 1973 for the Sunshine Family. The original baby was called Little Sweets. Barbie doll's dress, although not real buckskin, has an authentic look to it. I have put my doll on display in my husband's Western room, along with Pocahontas and Kokoum and the American Indians from the Dolls Of The World series (For additional information, see pages 112, 116, 121, *Barbie Exclusives Book II).*

Designed by: Sharon Zuckerman

15

Gold Jubilee
12009 • 1994 • $900

This doll is remarkable for several reasons. She is Mattel's second anniversary doll (the first Pink Jubilee 1989, was not produced through the Timeless Creations division). Gold Jubilee is beautiful and in high demand. Each Gold Jubilee is hand numbered in gold on the back. Mattel limited the number of pieces each store could acquire. This caused an unprecedented panic and in turn a savage demand. When shop-keepers and collectors alike didn't think they were going to get the best doll of the year, prices sky-rocketed to a high of $2,400. I myself paid more than they are now selling for. When resistance followed, prices plummeted. Even though the prices dropped considerably this doll still has great value. The closest Barbie doll in workmanship, design, and interest are any of the Bob Mackie Barbie dolls. Those who own Gold Jubilee are quite lucky.

Designed by: Carol Spencer

50th Anniversary of Mattel
#14479 • 1995 • $550

When it came time to celebrate Mattel's 50th Anniversary in 1996, Carol Spencer's assignment was to create the doll that everyone would want. She did. Not everyone wanted to pay the price, but the doll is well worth it. The porcelain doll's voluptuous red velvet and appropriately trimmed gold lamé combination is adorned with 50 roses, one for each year of Mattel's existence. The manufacturing materials make this irresistibly gorgeous doll hard to fit in a budget. Before production began on this doll, I told an executive in the Timeless Creation Division that I would prefer to see vinyl rather than porcelain because it would have been less expensive, thus allowing more people to share in Mattel's 50-year accomplishment.

Designed by: Carol Spencer

Starlight Waltz
#14070 • 1995 • $125

Starlight Waltz Barbie doll was the start of a new series. This doll was also made with brunette hair for the Doll and Bear Convention held at Disney World in Orlando, Florida. The designer of Starlight Waltz attended the convention to sign the dolls. The signature on these dolls would say Heather Dutton. She has since married and changed her name. The packaging is ideal for those who keep their dolls in the boxes. I think it is wonderful that Mattel is using the shoe box style packaging, and has taken it a step further by putting a sturdy plastic window on it to protect the doll and at the same time give full visibility to Starlight Waltz's dazzling beauty. I hope they will use this packaging more often.

Designed by: Heather Fonseca

18

Midnight Waltz
#15685 • 1996 • $100

Every photograph of Midnight Waltz's gown appeared black. In fact, her dress is a deep, deep midnight blue. I am happy to see that the window shoe box is used. It would be a pity not to be able to see this doll's magnificence. There were a couple of dolls designed for 1996 that have similar curls on top of their heads. There is a joke that these similar hairdo-ed dolls were released first so that the hair stylists could practice for perfection on Pink Splendor Barbie doll.

Designed by: Heather Fonseca

Starlight & Midnight Waltz Boxes

These boxes have Impressionistic art work which is as nice as the dolls.

Barbie Millicent Roberts

Matinee Today
#16079 • 1996 • $75

From now on, there shouldn't be a collector ever to ask again, "What is Barbie's full name?" Will this doll be the start of a whole new classification? I think so! I had put in a request a long time ago at Mattel for Barbie doll's parents, like the Heart Family Parents years ago. This would be the logical category to put them in. But I don't care even if it isn't logical ... she needs her Mommy and Daddy. Let's wait and see. As for what we have now, isn't Barbie Millicent Roberts great?!

We box removers really enjoy the dolls that have their own personal wardrobe. (See the next two pages.) BMR, as she is fondly referred to, is my favorite release for 1996. Her Chanel-inspired suit and accompanying fashions reflect the fashion industry's sentiments while capturing a truly new direction for the Barbie doll.

Designed by: Damaris Vidal

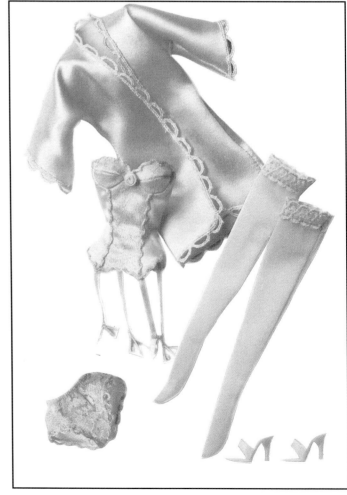

Goin' To The Game Fashion
#16076 • 1996 • $35

From the bleachers Barbie doll cheers on her favorite team. Over the years, Barbie doll has been a team player. I think she gets this from the design department, where women, and occasionally men, work together to come up with concepts and patterns to keep Barbie doll at the top of the fashion scene and tops in nation wide, if not world wide, sales.

Designed by: Nora Harri-Trezona

Picnic Perfect Fashion
16077 • 1996 • $35

You get a lot for your money when you buy this fashion. Picnic in the Park comes with little accessories: plates, silverware, glasses, napkins trimmed with lace, a blanket, shorts, tote, belt, hat shoes, two tops, shorts, skirt, and most importantly, no velcro! And no doll. You get to choose the doll YOU want to dress.

Designed by: Nora Harri-Trezona

Gold
5405 • 1990 • $975

Back in 1990, little did we know what a hot commodity the newly released Gold Bob Mackie doll was going to be. I opened my account with Mattel the year before. She was and still is the most wonderful doll to me. The doll came in a brown shipping carton with no outer box, and a Plexiglas™ display case with Bob Mackie's signature on it. Mattel later offered this same case separately without the signature. The shipping carton had foam to protect the lucite™ box in the carton. There is a place in the foam for the stand. My entire shipment was missing their stands. How was I going to sell them with the stands missing? My Mattel rep, Shirley Mallory, was going to have me send the dolls back. That meant I would have to wait a long time for replacements, and I didn't want to do that. I started packing them up when I realized that Mattel had put the disk part of the stand under her feet. What a relief! Later releases had the stands put into the foam slots. I love all Mackie dolls, but this is still my favorite. I think it's that first-born thing.

Assisted by: Janet Goldblatt
Designed by: Bob Mackie

Platinum
2703 • 1991 • $800

Mattel drastically changed the packaging with this release. The plastic case you see with the Gold doll was eliminated. Her gown has an abundance of white fish-scaled sequins, thickly layered and adorned with glass bugle beads and silver colored sequins at the neckline. Rhinestone drop ball earrings complete the sparkling ensemble. This was the first platinum hairdo Barbie doll had in a really long time.

Designed by: Bob Mackie

Platinum Blue
#2703 • 1991 • $1,200

Variations are always of particular interest to the diehard collector. This Platinum Barbie doll is referred to as the Blue Bob Mackie. It is not easy to see, but the sequins are blue. There is a lack of yellow sequins sewn on the gown. Under florescent lights at most doll shows, the true color is very difficult to see. The difference in the two gowns shows up better in natural lighting. Lucky is the collector who owns one!

Designed by: Bob Mackie

Starlight Splendor
#2704 • 1991 • $975

Starlight Splendor Barbie doll was originally named Midnight and then later changed by Mattel. Some of the early literature refers to this doll as Midnight and for a short while there were those who thought there was an additional doll in the series. When this doll first released, my select group of customers were resistant to buy it but my enthusiasm persuaded their purchase. Later, when the doll was no longer available and the value jumped considerably, anyone who bought it, was extremely grateful. I kept re-ordering the doll. Shirley Mallory, my rep at Mattel, was astonished by my actions as her other accounts were not buying the doll at all, much less re-ordering. I bet they wish they had!

Designed by: Bob Mackie

Starlight Pink
#2704 • 1991 • N/A

This has got to be one of the rarest of rarities. This Starlight Splendor is so unusual, that I didn't know what to make of it when one of my customers offered it to me. I had not heard anything about pink sequins, and when I asked other dealers they thought I was crazy. I took the doll to Judy Schizas at Mattel to see if she thought it was genuine. Being familiar with every aspect of Mattel production, she confirmed that it was authentic and that I was fortunate to have a unique variation. Now take another look at your doll and take your book with you. Good luck.

Designed by: Bob Mackie

Empress Bride
#4247 • 1992 • $1,200

The most expensive (based on original retail price) vinyl Barbie doll to come down the isle was the Empress Bride. The suggested retail was $250. In addition to her price, the diameter of her skirt had collectors thinking twice before adding her to their collection. Her skirt, with a multitude of crinoline underskirts takes up a lot of space. In celebration of Barbie doll's 35th anniversary, Disney had a special Barbie show at the Mattel-sponsored Barbie Festival held in Orlando, Florida. It included a real live "Barbie" wearing this gown. It must have weighed a ton.

Designed by: Bob Mackie

Neptune Fantasy
#4248 • 1992 • $1,200

Neptune Fantasy Barbie doll seems to be the most desirable in the series. Initially her production level was very low. There was a paper problem somewhere along the line. It was thought that all the dolls had been produced, when in fact they had not. Production on this doll was terminated, only to find out afterwards that they were short a lot of dolls. Mattel, after some deliberation, decided to re-tool. But when they did, they could not find the same fabric and beads at the original production price. In a hurry and determinated to keep the collector happy, Mattel came up with new fabric and sequins that would appear to be the same. There is a slight difference in the hand of the fabric that will trick the expert. I have not seen any concern or price variation as a result of this minor, undetectable difference. Anyone who owns either version is happy.

Designed by: Bob Mackie

Masquerade Ball
#10803 • 1993 • $595

It was originally planned that Masquerade Ball Barbie doll was to have been shipped with Mr. Mackie's new perfume, "Mackie", that was packaged in a box that matched the doll's gown. There were a few dolls that came into the United States with the perfume packaged in the box. Unfortunately this was stopped almost immediately because Mattel was afraid that the bottles would break in transit. The balance of the dolls were heavily scented instead. The masquerade ballgown is ornately patterned with an unusual color combination of bugle beads. This is not the first Barbie doll fashion to have a snood. Mattel used it on Guinevere's outfit in 1964.

Designed by: Bob Mackie

Queen of Hearts
#12046 • 1994 • $275

Everyone's sweetheart should have gotten one of these dolls for Valentine's Day. If they didn't, husbands and boyfriends still have an opportunity to do something wonderful for their sweetheart, as prices on this doll for the moment are still affordable. Queen of Hearts wonderfully luscious garnet red velvet cape, embroidered hearts around her cape, the abundance of sequins on her gown, her pitch-black hair, and a the touch of rhinestones so elegantly positioned, all make this doll irresistible.

Designed by: Bob Mackie

Goddess of the Sun
#14056 • 1995 • $250

Bob Mackie's Goddess of the Sun illuminates rays of happiness every time you look at her. Her golden hair distracts from her peek-a-boo bodice. Mr. Mackie used the same high quality beads and sequins as seen on his previous dolls. As with all the Bob Mackie dolls, she comes with her own stand and illustration. The earrings look familiar don't they? Barbie doll's monochromatic gown is gorgeous.

Designed by: Bob Mackie

Moon Goddess
#14105 • 1996 • $220

Bob Mackie's designs continue to be the most popular dolls for the collector. The opening price of these Mackie dolls has increased moderately each year, but not to the point of being intolerable. When you consider the elaborateness of the gowns, the unique face mold, the original face paint and superb packaging, as well as the probability of appreciation, how can you go wrong?
Designed by: Bob Mackie

* At the time of printing, Mattel was planning a Spring 1997 infomercial and the introduction of several new Bob Mackie dolls.

Rapunzel
#13016 • 1994 • $50

Rapunzel was nominated and won a DOTY® (Doll of the Year) Award in 1995. It was a shame that no one from Mattel was at the Doll and Bear Convention at Disney World to accept the award. Heather Dutton was at the Convention to sign her doll, Starlight Waltz, and was to have accepted the award, but at the last minute Mattel put her on a plane and sent her to the Orient. This series is a darling concept that mothers and daughters can share. The theme is one that small children can identify with and one that mothers want their children to have.

Designed by: Anne Bray

Little Bo Peep
#14960 • 1995 • $45

This is the first doll released that Nora Harri-Trezona has designed. Little Bo Peep is the second in the Children's Collector Series. She looks really cute in or out of the box and can help decorate a little girl's room. I heard a lot of adult collector opinions — they didn't like her white legs with painted ballerina shoes and they thought the doll should have had sheep. Some of them may not have remembered that Bo Peep had lost her sheep. I was able to come up with a supplier who manufactured sheep that were not only reasonable and the right scale, but fuzzy and jointed as well. I guess you could say they found each other in the end.

Designed by: Nora Harri-Trezona

Classique

Benefit Ball
#1521 • 1992 • $200

Mattel needed a line of dolls that would be attractive to the collector, fit most budgets, and would appeal to many tastes. For years Mattel did not share information about who was the designer of what. It was quite a surprise when they decided to incorporate in-house designers with the all-new Classique Collection. Each designer whose creativity went into a doll would be given public recognition. Benefit Ball was the first in the series with fabulous red hair. Or shall I say, that is how it was photographed. On Barbie doll's boat ride over from the Orient, her hair went limp from the humidity. So, if your doll's hair is looking a little flat, do what Carol Spencer told me to do: put some curlers in the hair and comb it up a bit; the doll will look fine. Mine didn't, but now she does, don't you think?

Designed by: Carol Spencer

Fifth Avenue Fashion
#1646 • 1992 • $55

To add interest to the grouping, Mattel added two fashions that were specifically for the Classique Collection. Barbie doll and her perfectly groomed, unnamed dog walk down 5th Avenue to get the Mattel Barbie Fashion Daily. If you are like me, you will need your magnifying glasses to read it. Barbie doll's suit is a wonderful suede cloth with a real zipper. All the Classique fashions have real zippers, snaps, hooks, and eyes. These findings make them a pleasure to dress and redress.

Designed by: Carol Spencer

Hollywood Premiere Fashion
#1618 • 1992 • $55

The second fashion in the Classique Collection is a fabulous two piece ensemble of chiffon and lamé. I have chosen a FAO Schwarz Winter Fantasy as seen on page 35 of *Barbie Exclusives Book I*, to model this perky party piece. The Mattel Timeless Creations catalog accidentally had the stock numbers reversed on the 1992 fashions. The numbers listed here are with the appropriate fashion.

Designed by: Carol Spencer

Opening Night
#10148 • 1993 • $150

After years of service, Janet Goldblatt was given recognition with Opening Night Barbie doll and the two fashions featured on the next page. (Don't turn yet!) Opening Night Barbie is a true black-hairdo doll with rooted eyelashes. What a knock-out! The earrings really show up well against the pitch black coif. The floor length gown of satin is topped with a jacket that is adorned with just the right number of sequins. The eyes were painted to match the bodice. It's all topped off with a simple but elegant evening hat. I think it is just the kind of ensemble Miss Goldblatt would wear herself. In fact, she did. She had this gown made to fit herself and wore it to the Baltimore Barbie Doll Convention in 1993.

Designed by: Janet Goldblatt

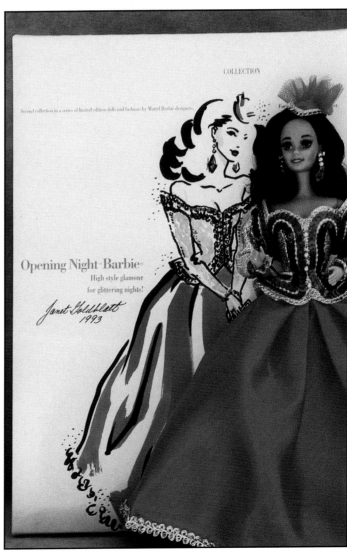

City Style
#10149 • 1993 • $135

City Style Barbie doll is costumed with European flair. A quilted handbag, faux pearl and chain necklace, and the monogrammed shopping bag Barbie doll carries could have come from Barbie doll's own boutique on Rodeo Drive in Beverly Hills. Underneath that fine fedora is a marvelously full head of hair. We don't get to see too many short hairdo dolls. This is the only doll in the Classique Collection that does not have rooted eyelashes. City Style Barbie doll was re-packaged and sold exclusively at Canada's Bay Department store.

Designed by: Janet Goldblatt

Uptown Chic
#11623 • 1993 • $80

Quite a few collectors missed out on this doll when she was first released. She was available mainly in the finer specialty shops. Most major stores did not offer her for sale, so those who don't order from doll stores might not have seen her. Uptown Chic's leatherette pantsuit is the only sportswear doll in the series. The snaps on the blouse often pop open making her a bit sexier than Mattel intended. This doll's eyelashes are lushly thick adding to her sex appeal.

Designed by: Kitty Black Perkins

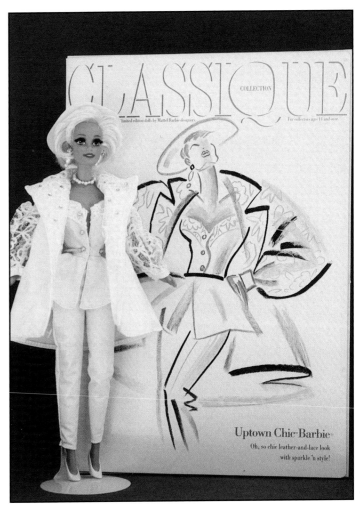

Flower Shower Fashion
#10150 • 1993 • $45

I selected the re-issued Italian doll to model Flower Shower Fashion. I felt that Barbie doll's skin tone, eyes, and make-up were perfect with the brilliant colors in the jacket. I am particularly fond of her hat. The fabric of the jacket is the same fabric we saw on Country Star Barbie doll for Walmart. See page 112 and 113, *Barbie Exclusives Book I*.

Designed by: Janet Goldblatt

Satin Dreams Fashion
#10151 • 1993 • $45

Janet Goldblatt also got to create the Opening Night doll's fashions. Barbie doll's lingerie has always been special. Janet Goldblatt's four piece peignoir has got to be the nicest, because the lace is so delicate and feminine. The detail is super. Barbie doll deserves elegant lingerie, so Janet selected a fine satin finished fabric and trimmed it with the finest lace she could find to accent Barbie doll's sleep wear.

Designed by: Janet Goldblatt

Extravaganza White
#11622 • 1993 • $80

Barbie doll's gown reminds me of a Busby Berkely movie from the 1930s. It is as dramatic as Barbie doll herself. Imagine her gliding across the stage. Kitty Black Perkins chose a fabric that was inexpensive but extremely effective.

Designed by: Kitty Black Perkins

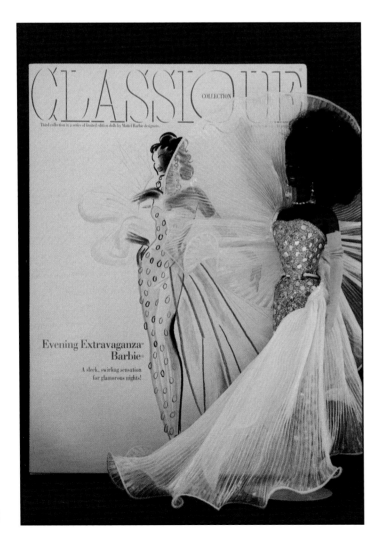

Extravaganza Black
#11638 • 1993 • $95

Black Extravaganza Barbie doll was not stocked well in all parts of the country. That is not unusual because black dolls don't usually sell as fast or in such large quantities. Not unlike the Bob Mackie Starlight Splendor, many collectors did not purchase her right away and when they returned to the store to get her, she was gone. I happen to prefer this doll to the white version. It is difficult to realize her appeal when she is left in her box on the blue-metallic liner. The color of the liner detracts from her beauty.

Designed by: Kitty Black Perkins

Extravaganza Black
#11638 • 1993 • $125

Variations are always a lot of fun. A few beads that became earrings for this doll were not clear. The earrings you see pictured here are a rare butterscotch amber color. Shani doll's boyfriend Jamal makes a handsome escort for Extravaganza Barbie doll.

Designed by: Kitty Black Perkins

Midnight Gala
#1299 • 1995 • $80

An extraordinary value! The velveteen fabric selected is printed with gold glitter paint. Her twisted hair, banded tightly at the top, reminds me of Jean Kasen on the TV show *Cheers*. Many collectors compare her to Masquerade Ball Barbie doll and to the limited edition FAO Schwarz Jewel Splendor. The beauty mark is not necessarily needed to determine her beauty. If it was, Mattel would have to put beauty marks on 99.9% of the Barbie dolls!

Designed by: Abbe Littleton

Starlight Dance White
#15461 • 1996 • $66

Glamour Barbie doll is constantly being compared to the fabulous FAO Schwarz doll, Silver Screen. Although the face mold doesn't resemble Silver Screen Barbie doll, the sumptuous pearl silk charmeuse does. Cut on the bias, as were gowns from the late 1930s, certainly shows off the doll's amazing physique. The sensuous bodice is delicately adorned with rhinestones and glitter which accent her headband, cuffs, and earrings. Barbie doll's platinum hair was also seen on the Platinum Mackie. This has to be one of the best values for 1996.

Designed by: Cynthia Young

Starlight Dance Black
#15819 • 1996 • $66

There are few dolls from the Barbie Collectibles division that are black dolls. Mattel was wise to choose the Nichelle face mold from 1993. Wearing the same color and style gown as the white version, Black Starlight Dance Barbie doll is just as simply understated. Those collectors who did not order her should pick this doll up while she is still reasonable. She is marvelous.

Designed by: Cynthia Young

Christian Dior
#13168 • 1995 • $200

The original plan for the Christian Dior doll had long hair. It was an almost last minute decision by Mattel to upsweep her hair, and is far more effective on such an elegant figure. The general consensus was that Mattel was charging a bit too much for the doll. Some other collectors complained about the color of the box. Several of those I spoke with who didn't like the silver book box did not realize that The House of Dior's trademark color was being used. It was the appropriate choice for this couturier doll.

Designed by: Janet Goldblatt

Photograph courtesy of Mattel, Inc.

Christian Dior-50th Anniversary
#16013 • 1996 • $180

Mattel and Dior celebrate the House of Dior's 50th anniversary with Barbie doll dressed in a replica 1947 ensemble. Barbie doll's champagne colored silk shantung sparkles. The knife pleated skirt is of fine wool crepe with a tulle petticoat. Accessories include faux pearl necklace, bracelet, earrings, classic pumps, black gloves, stockings, and a garter to help hold them up. Barbie doll's face is absolutely gorgeous. It has a wonderful porcelain look. To emphasize glamour, the doll has a small beauty mark. The dolls from the House of Dior are extremely elegant and were only available at specialty stores.

Designed by: Dior
Adapted by: Robert Best

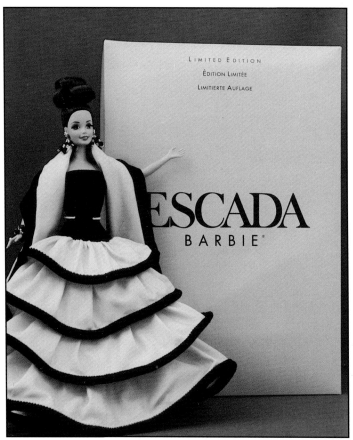

Escada
#15948 • 1996 • $190

There has been some question as how to classify this doll. Is this the start of a new series called European Designers or is it continuing the Designer series? I consider the doll a follow up to the Christian Dior doll. The doll is so stunning that it could go anywhere. The silk gown is a reproduction of an early one from the House of Escada in Europe. Barbie doll's beautiful brown eyes were painted to match the upswept hair. The black beaded earrings fill the space of the doll's elegant neckline and fall just above the silk-lined stole to keep its shoulders warm on the way to the opera. Don't be bothered by the slubs in the fabric! The slubs prove it is genuine silk.

Adapted by: Janet Goldblatt

Empress Sissy
#15846 • 1996 • $160

Empress Sissy Barbie doll's ball gown can be seen on a 19th century painting by Franz Xavier Winter Hatler. This royal gown is a recreation inspired by Austria's Empress Sissy. The first time this doll was seen was at the Barbie Festival in Orlando, Florida.

Stardust Costume I
#10993 • 1994 • $800

How a toy company ever got the rights to produce a work of art beats me, but Mattel did! The Erté porcelains are under license with Louise Westergarrd Productions, Inc., and Sevenarts, Ltd. Aren't we lucky to be able to see and own a work of art designed by one of the most renowned artists of all time, Erté. Using the finest porcelain, Mattel did a spectacular job. When Mattel first unveiled Stardust, Barbie doll collectors were confused; many presumed it was a Barbie doll. In fact, I don't understand why Erté's work is being referred to as a doll. Doulton and Limouge don't call their figurines dolls. Doll by definition is a toy. I would hardly call this a toy. Would you?

Designed by: Erté
Adapted by: Janet Goldblatt

Stardust Costume II
#14109 • 1996 • $700

Born into a family of Russian decent, Erté designed his first gown for his mother at the age of five. His career spanned decades of cover designs for fashion magazines and costuming for the theater and films. In his later years he turned to sculpture, jewelry, and wearable art. Many have never had the opportunity to experience Erté. Now, because of Mattel, some are fortunate enough not only to see some of his work but actually own it too. From the first time I saw these porcelains, I did not understand why they were being offered to doll shops instead of art galleries. They are definitely works of art. This, the second in a series, and like so many of Mattel's other products, experienced a considerable price increase. Price is not to be confused with value. This Erté is the best value offered in the 1996 catalog.

Designed by: Erté
Adapted by: Janet Goldblatt

Photograph courtesy of Mattel, Inc.

Great Eras Collection

Back Row (Left to Right): Elizabethan Queen, 1850's Southern Belle, Gibson Girl, Medieval Lady. *Front Row* (Left to Right): Victorian Lady, 1920's Flapper, Grecian Goddess, Egyptian Queen.

Gibson Girl
#3702 • 1993 • $150

The Great Eras Collection is a great value. Collectors have to have every one. The Gibson Girl seemed to take a while to catch on. The theme was a departure from the normal Barbie doll fashion. Historically, this ensemble is an accurate depiction of a Charles Dana Gibson illustration. Gibson was a famous painter and illustrator from the late 1800s. It was his fashion work that gave rise to the expression Gibson Girl. The moiré fabric and high collar blouses were widely used for a few short years. Throughout the Great Eras Collection, Carol Spencer, has given great thought to historic accuracy in every detail. I look forward to more in the future.

Designed by: Carol Spencer

1920's Flapper
#4063 • 1993 • $250

The roaring twenties is my favorite fashion era. Almost every one who looks at this doll immediately thinks of *The Great Gatsby*, Bonnie and Clyde, and the Black Bottom. This 1920s influenced doll is about as cute as you can get. No detail, no accessory has been overlooked. The doll looks ready to dance the Charleston. I love it! This doll has it all and is my favorite in the series. Which one is yours?

Designed by: Carol Spencer

Egyptian Queen
#11397 • 1993 • $150

Many collectors compare the Egyptian Queen to Elizabeth Taylor in Cleopatra. Some were bothered about the eye paint. I sometimes wonder if the doll had been named Egyptian Princess instead of Queen, would collectors have been happier with this doll? When Mattel announced its release, I think there were those of us who had a preconceived idea of what this doll was going to look like. I had a vision of a remake of the Fashion Queen Barbie doll from 1964. I had to look at Egyptian Queen Barbie doll for several weeks before I got over my vision of what I thought she was going to be. The face paint is unusual; the gown is extraordinarily delicate. Should you decide to take the doll out of its box, be extremely careful because the delicate chiffon snags easily.

Designed by: Carol Spencer

1850's Southern Belle
#11478 • 1993 • $150

There are several Barbie dolls named Southern Belle or Southern Beauty, so if you want to mail order this doll, make sure you tell the seller that you want the one from the Great Eras Collection or you could end up with a Sears® doll. I would not have thought to choose pink and blue for this period piece. It was not a common color combination for the 1800s but it does suit the doll. Barbie doll's ensemble is elaborately constructed right down to her petticoat. Another wonderful value.

Designed by: Carol Spencer

Medieval Lady
#12791 • 1994 • $95

When I look at Medieval Barbie doll's dress it reminds me sooooo much of the one done for Barbie doll in 1964 that I often start reminiscing about the good old days. The dress is a deep amethyst velveteen. Barbie doll's period piece is simply constructed with just the right amount of adornment that was typical of those days. I love the snood. I want one for myself, even though they probably don't sell them anymore. Too bad, they were practical and could easily disguise a real bad hair day, not that Barbie doll ever has bad hair days.

Designed by: Carol Spencer

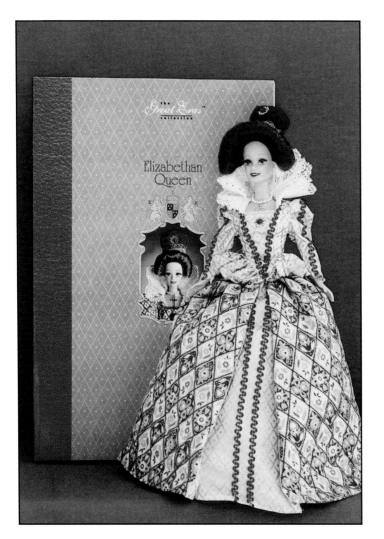

Elizabethan Queen
#12792 • 1994 • $75

Not the most beautiful face. NO, it's not. Queen Elizabeth the First was no Barbie doll either. So in the future when non-Barbie doll collectors go on and on about how Barbie doll's image as a raging beauty is damaging, show them this doll. Although she is not what we expect from seeing her predecessors, she is something special in her own right. The fabric choice and style is historically accurate and is certainly a departure from the old cliché that all Barbie dolls look alike.

Designed by: Carol Spencer

Grecian Goddess
#15005 • 1995 • $65

I thought all Barbie dolls were goddesses, so what makes this one so special that goddess is in her name? It's because her fashion was specifically modeled after Athena, the goddess of learning, wisdom, and protector of Ancient gold. Hence, Barbie doll's elaborate gold-tone laurel leaf collar, belt, and headpiece. If you were wondering, as my friend and I were, about whether or not Barbie doll's curls were rooted or attached to her headpiece, let me assure you that they are rooted. The crystal pleated dress is outlined with gold color thread and the skirt is overlaid with illusion that is sprinkled with golden glitter to give it an added touch of elegance.

Designed by: Carol Spencer

Victorian Lady
#14900 • 1995 • $65

The first doll in the series to cover the 1800s was Southern Belle, which portrayed a very southern woman wearing a spring/summer fashion. With Victorian Lady, however, we see a very northern winter look. Barbie doll's plush garnet velvet dress trimmed with ecru lace and a bustle must have been difficult for the sewers to construct. The ensemble is topped off with a darling hat with a tuft of marabou and tied at the chin, with a satin ribbon. The only thing I find disturbing is the jewelry. It is more likely that the earrings would have been real rose-cut diamonds. Don't I wish! Note that the box date is 1995, but this Victorian was not released until the summer of 1996.

Designed by: Carol Spencer

Who has never seen the wonderful classic *Gone With The Wind*? The Hollywood Legends Series was a wonderful new direction for Barbie doll and Mattel. A new license agreement with Ted Turner and Mattel began another Barbie doll phenomenon. Mattel's new infomercial would compete for sales with their own best customers, the specialty stores. Many new collectors did not realize they could select their own doll at their local doll store. The infomercial brought great new awareness to the collectiblity of the doll, allowing Mattel a greater net profit on each doll by retailing rather than wholesaling. The Scarlet doll in the white gown was never shown on the infomercial. Some collectors missed out because they didn't know about her. Don't they look wonderful together?

Scarlett Green Velvet
#12045 • 1994 • $110

Barbie doll's green velvet dress is from a memorable scene in *Gone With the Wind*. You might recall that this is the dress Scarlett made from the curtains to meet Rhett in Atlanta. Mattel's adaptation of this gown and doll was so well received that collectors were biting at the bit for the rest of the series.

Adapted by: Carol Spencer

Scarlett in Red Dress
#12815 • 1994 • $110

Another memorable scene (which scene isn't memorable?) occurred when Rhett made Scarlett attend the party in her scarlett red velvet gown. This doll was my best store seller in the series. There had been talk about the earrings in the first releases being real gold. Has anyone had their earrings tested for real gold? I can't see a difference. There had also been talk about an open mouthed version which made Scarlett too smiley for the emotional scene she was portraying in this gown. I have never seen a smiling red Scarlett.

Adapted by: Carol Spencer

Scarlett Bar-b-que
#12997 • 1994 • $75

Next to be released was Scarlett's dress from the picnic scene. There were a couple of hardly noticeable changes on this doll and her packaging. The dolls that were to be sent out direct from the mail order division were packaged individually in their own shipping cartons. When Mattel had excess dolls in the mail order division they started sending them to the stores. At some point, Scarlett's hair was repositioned. The first releases had her hair spread. Later releases had her hair coming downward, filling her neckline. The dye lots on the velvet trim vary in shades of green, and there are two different straw hats known to exist.

Adapted by: Carol Spencer

Scarlett Honeymoon
#13254 • 1994 • $95

There had been talk that Mattel was going to make Scarlett's wedding gown. The project was scratched and we went right to Scarlett's honeymoon. Her dress could not be more accurate. The fine cut-out on the sleeves and delicate lace shawl make this a stunning combination. What a handsome couple Ken doll as Rhett and Barbie doll as Scarlett make.

Adapted by: Carol Spencer

Rhett Butler
#12741 • 1994 • $85

Ken doll has always been secondary for collectors, but Rhett is not secondary to Scarlett. I think this is one of the best Ken dolls Mattel has ever produced. He is particularly handsome in his vintage costume. There was one minor problem that you might want to attend to. His hat has a black band inside which bleeds onto Rhett's head. You might consider lining the inside so that the dye does not adhere to his forehead. I am told that some have used a special tape; I used tissue paper.

Adapted by: Carol Spencer

Dorothy Wizard of Oz
#12701 • 1994 • $75

It seems there were more variations on this doll than any other to date. The original photos from Mattel showed Barbie doll without braids. In the movie Judy Garland had braids, so production was held up while Dorothy's hair was being braided. Originally Toto had a red and white blanket in her basket. There was no blanket in the movie, so they quit putting it in the package. They were not happy with the shade of blue gingham that was selected, so that changed and now we have both light and dark blue versions. One of the most interesting and least talked about changes was in the eye paint. I have given you close-ups of both; one has white reflectors and the other has tan. Note that this box is all cardboard.

Adapted by: Abbe Littleton

Dorothy Wizard of Oz
#12701 • 1995 • $50

Mattel decided to change the boxes for the Tin Man and for Glinda. They would be packaged with hard plastic tops like the holiday dolls. After making this decision, Mattel felt that Dorothy deserved the same consideration. So they redesigned her box, gave her a floral front border and hard plastic top to match Glinda's and the Tin Man's, and put a new date on the box. This one says 1995 but was released in 1996. For collectors who keep their dolls in the box, a hard plastic top is almost mandatory. Since I take my dolls out, normally I would not care, but for some reason I have decided to buy a hard plastic top to keep in my collection for show and tell.

Adapted by: Abbe Littleton

Glinda Wizard of Oz
#14901 • 1995 • $85

Glinda, not Glenda, a common mistake, has one of the fullest skirts we have ever seen. The gown is an authentic replica of the gown used in the original movie. There was an unfortunate delay in her release because the first batch of dolls to come into the United States was wearing a less elaborate dress with no jewels and less ornamentation. She was well worth the wait.

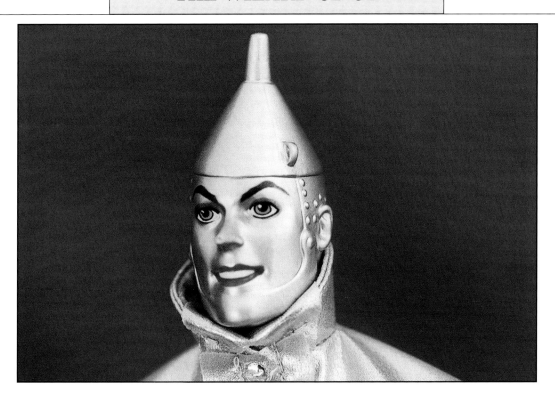

Tin Man Wizard of Oz
#14902 • 1995 • $85

I was delighted to see Mattel use a jointed Ken doll to make the Tin Man. Joints allow more flexibility when making a display. The Tin Man's outfit was constructed from many seamed pieces. Underneath his suit of "tin" is a one piece body suit. (I guess that is so the faux metal doesn't chafe him.) Underneath that is silver colored plastic. The plastic appears to be poured that way. The doll comes complete with ax, oil can, and heart.

Maria
#13676 • 1995 • $55

With all the characters in the movie *The Sound of Music*, isn't it odd that Mattel only produced one doll? Thank goodness; if we had to buy all the children that were in the film, we would all be in the poor house. This doll did not sell as well as I thought she would. I can't explain it because she is really cute. Her hat is suspiciously like Little Debbie's. See page 53 of *Barbie Exclusives, Book I*. There must have been a shortage of lace, because there was a change. The photo, on page 79, shows that the flowers on the petticoat lace are larger than on the first releases.

Adapted by: Janet Goldblatt

Maria & Dorothy
Variation Photo

Eliza Pink & Professor Higgins Photo

My Fair Lady
MFL #1 Pink Gown
#15501 • 1995 • $85

It is sad that Audrey Hepburn couldn't be here to see Barbie doll wearing the costumes that she wore in *My Fair Lady*. As Eliza Doolittle, Barbie doll outdoes herself. Her gown is the airiest chiffon and the boa is so romantic that Eliza blushes with femininity. The rooted eyelashes and face paint are just the right amount to accent the ensemble. Although the date on these boxes say 1995, the dolls were not released until 1996.*

Adapted by: Janet Goldblatt

*The box date is the copyright notice and may not be the same year the product was released in abundance in the stores.

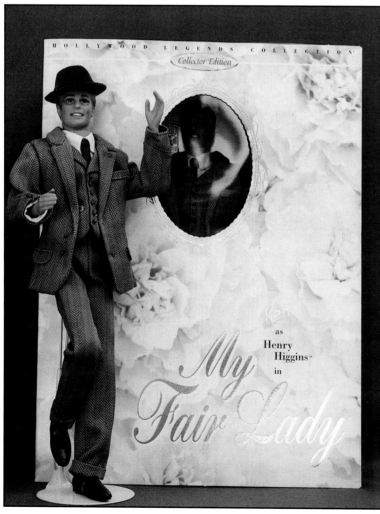

Professor Higgins
#15499 • 1995 • $82

I thought Ken doll as Rhett Butler was the best, until Professor Higgins was released. It was a tough decision, but I think Professor Higgins is a little better. He is fully posable, with bendable legs and jointed elbows. Isn't he wonderful? His suit alone is worth the money. Professor Higgin's wonderful herringbone-like jacket is completely lined and trimmed with fourteen beaded buttons. A pocket square in the breast pocket, grosgrain tie, and wonderful hat complete this stunningly handsome ensemble. The hat shown in the early promotional photos was a wool herringbone hat. The copy specifically refers to it as wool, but in the end the hat is a solid taupe colored, molded faux felt hat. This is a new face mold for Ken doll. There are smile lines and wrinkles around his eyes. Look closely at them. Some claimed that Professor Higgins is wearing new shoes, but no, these are the same shoes used on the porcelain Ken doll.

Adapted by: Sharon Zuckerman

MFL # 2 Ascot
#15497 • 1995 • $85

After being groomed by Professor Higgins, Eliza Doolittle attends the Ascot races. This is her first society appearance. She could not have worn a more striking ensemble than this elegantly laced gown. The extremely ornate wide brim chapeau is to die for. This fabulous creature comes with a doll stand, shoes, gloves, matching parasol, and certificate of authenticity, as do all the others in the series.

Adapted by: Robert Best

MFL # 3 Flower Girl
#15498 • 1996 • $85

This costume is darling, isn't it? Eliza's multi-piece suit is made of the same velvet that we saw on the 1995 foreign holiday doll. This is the attire that Audrey Hepburn wore in the opening scene of Lerner and Lowe's musical *My Fair Lady*, back in 1964. Barbie doll carries a basket of violets from the Covent Garden. The color of the plastic was changed, but this same basket was used by Pilgrim Barbie doll to carry her corn; see page 11.

Adapted by: Carol Spencer

MFL #4 Embassy Ball
#15500 • 1996 • $110

It's the evening of the Embassy Ball, and Barbie doll as Eliza Doolittle could not have been more magnificent than in this wonderful gown of illusion and lace, sprinkled with rhinestones and bugle beads to match the tiara. No lady of the times would have attended a ball without the finishing touch of long white gloves.

Adapted by: Damaris Vidal

CELEBRATING 35 YEARS

35th Anniversary
Box Close-Ups

35th Anniversary Blonde Curved
#15590 • 1993 • $75

Mattel started planning Barbie doll's 35th birthday years in advance. They would need to come up with something spectacular to recapture the hearts of the now grown-up little girls. Ideas and concepts were bantered around. They would reproduce the doll that started it all, back in 1959, the #1 Barbie doll. The first releases had curved eyebrows. Mattel realized that this was not the true brow on a #1 and changed it. Rather than hold up the demand for these dolls, they decided to release the dolls with curved eyebrows anyway.

Designed by: Karen Victor

35th Anniversary Blonde V-Brow
#15590 • 1993 • $95

The 1959 Barbie doll looked more like this photo. Mattel's thinking was to have it look similar to the #1, but not identical, so that the novice collector could not be tricked into paying a vintage price on a repro doll. Therefore the exact mold was not used and PVC plastic was used, rather than original type vinyl. Her toes were rounded and her hair was made of silky saran rather than the early mohair-type saran. The 35th Anniversary is stamped 1958 in numbers, rather than the original Roman numerals.

Designed by: Karen Victor

35th Anniversary Brunette Curved
#11782 • 1993 • $75

The original #1 Barbie doll was sold in either blonde or brunette. The photo on the back of the early box releases of the brunettes had an interesting flaw. There is what appears to be a hair over her left eye. To amend the problem, Mattel tried to doctor the photo, but the line in the later releases, although more faint can still be seen.

Designed by: Karen Victor

35th Anniversary Brunette V-Brow
#11782 • 1993 • $125

These dolls in fact, are more like a #2 than a #1. None of them have holes in their feet. (The original was made with holes to accommodate her stand.) Mattel included with these dolls an original style swimsuit, sunglasses, shoes and a plastic stand that looks nothing like Barbie doll's original black metal stand.

Designed by: Karen Victor

35th Anniversary Blonde Gift Set
#11591 • 1993 • $175

And they said it can't be done! Well here is the proof that Mattel can make quality outfits at an affordable price. The two fashions included in this gift set are wonderfully accurate and detailed. (They are two of Barbie doll's three rarest outfits.) The ensemble on the left is the reproduction of the 1959 fashion called Roman Holiday.

The gift set included the doll's accessories: glasses, glass case, comb, necklace, shoes, hanky, belt, hat, purse, and even the illusive compact. Each Nostalgic doll comes with the 35th anniversary wrist tag. On the right hand side you see another repro fashion, Easter Parade. Included in this set is: the coat, dress, hat, purse, and necklace. I have chosen a brunette to model the Roman Holiday outfit. This doll was not available in the gift set. To learn more about the brunette gift set, see page 162, *Barbie Exclusives Book II.*
Adapted by: Karen Victor

Here are the original 1959 Barbie dolls dressed in the original Roman Holiday and Easter Parade ensembles. These are two of my favorite #2s.

Busy Gal

#136575 • 1995 • $100

As a child my most favorite outfit for my Barbie doll was the reproduction you see here called Busy Gal. I wanted it in the worst way. The reproduction came with all the same accessories as the original — body suit, jacket, skirt, belt, hat, open toe shoes, fashion portfolio, and two etchings. Note the difference in the bangs from the preceding dolls in this category. The bangs are curly. This is how the vintage dolls are. Busy Gal Barbie doll was mostly sold in specialty stores. Those who didn't work with a specialty store in securing their dolls had a harder time finding her in certain parts of the country.

Adapted by: Karen Victor

Solo In The Spotlight Blonde
#13534 • 1994 • $50

Solo in the Spotlight was my Barbie doll's favorite evening dress. I am surprised that more vintage collectors didn't buy this doll just to get the reproduction microphone. The originals were made of brittle plastic and are prone to breaking. The authentic microphone is quite pricey today.

Adapted by: Karen Victor

Solo In The Spotlight Brunette
#13820 • 1994 • $50

For Barbie doll's 36th birthday collectors got a repro of the 1960 Ponytail doll. The original 1960 dolls are referred to as #3's and #4's. To learn more about the early dolls you will need a copy of Sybil De Wein's *Collector's Encyclopedia of Barbie Dolls & Collectibles*. Vintage collectors refer to this book as "the Bible of Barbie dolls". I wake up thanking Sybil every day for writing it. If you decide you like vintage dolls, you will too.

Adapted by: Karen Victor

Enchanted Evening Blonde
#14992 • 1995 • $40

Every little girl in the 1960s had their favorite evening gown for her doll. Enchanted Evening was my cousin Joleen's favorite. When we played the Barbie board game Queen of the Prom, my cousin Joleen always chose this dress, and I always chose Solo. Many vintage collectors voiced their opinion that they would rather have seen this gown done in a darker pink tone. Either way, she is enchanting. The release of the Enchanted Evening dolls was in 1996.

Adapted by: Karen Victor

Enchanted Evening Brunette
#15407 • 1995 • $40

Enchanted Evening Barbie doll in brunette hair was just as popular as her platinum sister which Mattel called blonde. Both dolls sold very well. Barbie doll came with the accessories that were similar to the originals. They included her three strand necklace, long white gloves, fur stole, earrings (although the original was different than what you see here), and clear open toe slingbacks with glitter on them.

Adapted by: Karen Victor

Francie
#14808 • 1996 • $75

Francie, Barbie doll's cousin is a doll many recent collectors do not appreciate. It's sad that they did not experience Francie, especially because this is the best reproduction vinyl doll that Mattel has produced to date. This Francie doll copies the original so closely it is downright frightening. The main difference is the texture of her hair and her Malaysia stamp. I love this doll. I bought a lot of them for my own collection because I have a lot of Francie doll's early fashions and don't have enough dolls to model the clothes.

Adapted by: Karen Victor

Poodle Parade
#15280 • 1996 • $75

The American Girl Barbie doll was introduced in 1965. One year later Mattel produced an ensemble for her, and named it Poodle Parade. After 30 years, Mattel re-introduced both the doll and one of collectors' favorite fashions complete with all the accessories. The American Girl doll, with her new bend-leg mechanism was revolutionary. Other manufacturers would soon follow suit. I hope that all of you are having as much fun with your repro dolls as I am.

Adapted by: Karen Victor

Star Trek
#15006 • 1996 • $95

I predict that this gift set may go down in history as the most sought after gift set of all time. Trekers as well as Barbie doll collectors do and will want this set for years to come. I had a little fun with it. I took my Black Barbie doll from the 1980s and dressed her in Barbie doll's costume so that I could have an Ohura. It started a lot of trouble because everyone wanted to buy my doll. If you want an Ohura, you can do what I did, or wait till Mattel makes one. They might.

Adapted by: Robert Best

Blue Rhapsody
#1708 • 1986 • $700

More than a decade has passed since Mattel offered the first porcelain Barbie doll. They chose the Super Star Barbie doll face mold, created her own special glitter gown and made only 7,500 pieces. I was not aware of this doll till years after she had been retired. The Barbie doll network was not as developed then as it is today. This caliber Barbie doll was not available in Santa Barbara and I didn't know it existed, much less how I could order it. I had to buy the first three porcelains on the secondary market and have never regretted doing so.

Designed by: Kitty Black Perkins

Enchanted Evening
#3415 • 1987 • $325

Mattel used the pattern to this gown five times. It was originally created for the 1960 ponytail Barbie doll. It was sold in a package as a dress only or on a boxed dress doll. In 1987 it was used on the porcelain doll as you see here. Finally, in 1996, the pattern appeared for the fourth and fifth time on the blonde and brunette vinyl reproduction ponytail dolls.

Designed by: Carol Spencer

Wedding Day
#2621 • 1989 • $600

This is possibly the porcelain collector's most favorite doll. Wedding Day Barbie doll was released in two different shades of blonde. Here is the rarer of the two. Mattel chose this 1959 gown and gave the doll the 1959 face that so many of us remember from our childhood. The wedding gown is a recreation of Barbie doll's first bridal gown. The chantilly lace was updated with iridescent glitter and her corsage was designed larger than the original.

Designed by: Janet Goldblatt

Benefit Performance
#5475 • 1988 • $475

Benefit Performance Barbie doll was the first porcelain Barbie doll I discovered. When I saw her at a toy store I was so surprised and pleased that I ran to the bank to get money. If I had to pick a favorite, this would be the one, because she was my first porcelain. She was adapted from a 1967 Twist 'n Turn Barbie doll. This gown is strikingly similar to the original, but the jewelry is very different from the authentic one.

Designed by: Janet Goldblatt

Solo in the Spotlight
#7613 • 1990 • $250

Mattel liked dressing the Barbie doll porcelains in vintage gowns (five of the six dolls in the series would all be wearing previously-produced floor length gowns). Here we have Solo in the Spotlight from 1961, another all-time favorite. The original Solo In The Spotlight was sold as a fashion only or as a dressed box doll.

Designed by: Janet Goldblatt

Sophisticated Lady
#5313 • 1990 • $220

The last in the series is this wonderful comeback of Sophisticated Lady. It is unbelievable that this doll after all this time is still a sleeper. With vintage American Girls being as popular as they are, this doll should have appreciated more than she has, especially because her hairdo is a side part. Side parts are rare and are important to the vintage collector. Except for the fact that all the porcelains are slightly larger and the accessories are often different, the porcelain fashions are all virtually identical to the original vinyl dolls.

30th Anniversary Ken
#1110 • 1991 • $250

Ken doll was introduced to Barbie doll in 1961. The guy has been hanging around ever since. In honor of his birthday, Mattel recreated this fuzzy-headed image in porcelain. They appropriately selected the original tuxedo. His attire is such that he can be the ultimate escort for any of the other porcelains. This Ken doll has existed for a long time and his value has not budged. Ken has always been secondary to the Barbie doll when it comes to purchasing. I understand this, but cannot understand why, after all this time, he hasn't been included in more private collections. Each of the girl dolls should have an escort, especially the bride, but most collectors don't visualize the doll on display.

Designed by: Carol Spencer

PORCELAIN ANNIVERSARY DOLLS

30th Anniversary Midge
#7957 • 1992 • $220

Midge, Barbie doll's best friend, didn't release until 1963. Thirty years later we celebrated her birthday with this fabulous porcelain reproduction. This vintage reproduction Midge doll is wearing an all-time popular fashion called Senior Prom from 1963. Mattel added a corsage and a faux mink stole that was not with this dress originally and created an all-new necklace for the occasion.

Designed by: Carol Spencer

30th Anniversary Skipper
#11396 • 1993 • $220

From the moment I first saw this doll, I immediately determined that it was the best porcelain that Mattel had created — fabulous facial paint, great hair, and a perfect dress. The anniversary dress is a remake of Skipper doll's 1965 outfit called Happy Birthday. When Mattel brought Skipper back in 1994 they gave the doll all the original birthday girl accessories — a cake, party favors, napkin, an invitation, and even a present. These little bonuses make this doll that much more special.

Designed by: Carol Spencer

Gay Parisienne
#7526 • 1991 • $275

The original 1959 Barbie doll had three outfits that were very expensive and today are considered rare. The ensemble called Gay Parisienne was brought back and dressed on this porcelain in 1991. This was the first in a series of cocktail dresses for Barbie doll. This was the first porcelain Barbie doll to be made in more than one hair color. To learn more about other hair colors refer to the Disney Exclusives section of *Barbie Exclusives Book I*, pages 18-31.

Designed by: Carol Spencer

Silken Flame
#1249 • 1992 • $225

This porcelain Barbie doll was actually a combination of two separate outfits originally designed for the vinyl doll. Silken Flame was the name of the dress and was offered to the public in 1960. The red velvet coat was not on the market until the following year and was named Red Flare. The two were combined and dressed on this reproduction bubble cut. The quality of the dress and coat is as good as it was in 1960. This doll was also released in extremely limited numbers as a blonde. See the Disney section of *Barbie Exclusives Book I*, pages 18-31, for additional information.

Designed by: Carol Spencer

Plantation Belle
#7526 • 1991 • $225

This is the least historically accurate porcelain that Mattel put together. The dress and accessories, although very attractive and a popular vintage ensemble, are not what a Swirl Barbie doll would have worn. (Swirl refers to her hair-do.) The original Plantation Belle fashion was on the market from 1959 to 1961. The Swirl hair-do that Mattel selected for this porcelain did not come on the market until 1964. Barbie doll looks charming, but for a chronological fanatic like myself, the miss-matched combination of fashion and doll is distracting.

Designed by: Karen Victor

Prima Ballerina

Swan Lake
#1648 • 1991 • $225

In 1991 Mattel released the first of this series, a fabulous Swan Lake Barbie doll with elaborately twisted hair with iridescent strands, topped with a tuft of marabou. The doll came with a stand that inserted into the music box. The first stands were short and did not adequately hold up the doll. Stores could order replacements. Unfortunately, these replacement stands were not great either.

Designed by: Carol Spencer

Nutcracker
#5472 • 1991 • $195

Mattel made new arms for the ballerinas. Collectors did not respond well to the new hands with split fingers. When the series stopped, Mattel still had some of these arms left over and used them on the Gibson Girl dolls. See page 59. Each of the Ballerinas came with a music box stand which played as Barbie doll danced and a plastic cylinder to protect her. Thanks to Diane Fitch for having these for me.

Designed by: Carol Spencer

*Technically this doll is classified as one of the American Beauties but because of her costume, many collectors include her as part of the Stars 'n Stripes collection. See page 9 for additional information on this doll. *Photograph courtesy of Mattel, Inc.*

Air Force
#3360 • 1990 • $60

Air Force Barbie doll is technically the first in the series for Stars 'n Stripes. She is not, technically, the first military doll. To see the first armed forces doll in this grouping, turn to page 9, under American Beauties. Mattel changed the category after only two dolls. Barbie doll is wearing an official A-2 leather-like flight jacket. It is what a captain in the United States Air Force would wear. In order to go forward with all the dolls in the Stars 'n Stripes series, Mattel obtained permission to utilize logos, uniforms, and names from each branch of the services.

Navy White
#9693 • 1990 • $45

According to the box that Navy Barbie doll comes in, she has already been in the Navy for eight years. This means that she enlisted in the year 1982. The doll is wearing an official Navy uniform adorned with an authentic insignia and campaign ribbons. Her rank is that of quarter master and petty officer first class. Everything Barbie doll does is first class, we knew that!

Navy Black
#9694 • 1990 • $30

Both the white and black dolls come with an extra military pair of pants. This would qualify these dolls as gift sets. You also get black flats, a nautical map, labels, and cutouts which consist of sextant, compass, binoculars, camera, and log book.

Marine Barbie White
#7549 • 1991 • $35

Barbie doll left the United States Navy in 1991 to join the Marine Corps. As a Sergeant, Barbie doll received three medals as seen on her jacket. The authentic uniform is Dress Blues for enlisted women. This is what is worn for official formal Marine Corps events, family visits, and parades.

Marine Ken White
#7574 • 1991 • $55

The hardest doll in the series to find is Marine Corps Ken. Mattel used a new face mold, but did not give him a hair cut that would meet with the Marines high standards. They did not approve and Marine Corps' Ken doll was immediately discontinued. Consequently he was in limited supplies and hard to come by. We could say that he got kicked out for insubordination!

Marine Barbie Black
#7594 • 1991 • $30

Black Marine Corps Barbie doll's medals are the same as the white doll's. Both wear the Achievement Medal for actions above and beyond the call of duty. This doll proudly wears the Desert Storm Medal and a Good Conduct Medal that indicates three years of honorable service. We wouldn't expect anything less from Barbie now, would we?

Marine Ken Black
#5352 • 1991 • $30

Black Marine Corps Ken doll did not have the same problems that his buddy had. Black Ken doll's hair was short enough to meet the Marine Corps' requirements. The doll makes a pretty handsome soldier.

Marine Gift Set White
#4704 • 1991 • $90

The white gift sets are scarce for the same reason as the single Ken doll. The dolls in the gift sets are the same as the single dolls. They make a handsome couple, don't they?

Marine Gift Set Black
#N/A • 1991 • $60

Once again the dolls are the same in the gift set as in the single dolls. Mattel sometimes creates gift sets, but the production numbers are considerably lower.

Stars 'n Stripes Collection

Army Barbie White
#1234 • 1992 • $30

The air war in Iraq had the world's attention and so did Mattel. Wearing an authentic camouflage dress uniform of the desert battle, Sergeant Barbie doll of the 101st Airbourne Division, is dressed as a medic. Oops! Due to an oversight, Mattel did not have clearance from the Red Cross organization to utilize their symbol on her bag and removed the cross. As a result, only the early releases bore the cross.

Army Ken White
#1237 • 1992 • $30

Ken doll has the same sergeant status as Barbie doll. The insignia on Barbie doll's hat is that of a medic, while Ken doll's has the 101st Airborne unit insignia. The logo says "Rendez vous with Destiny". Ken doll's shoulder bag appears to be in the shape of a holster, yet there is no mention whatsoever of a gun.

Army Barbie Black
#5618 • 1992 • $25

New releases, after the cross oversight, had the doll holding the medic bag with the emblem pushed behind her hip so that it didn't show. Mattel put a special sticker over the cross on the back of the box. Earlier models are still in circulation.

Army Ken Black
#5619 • 1992 • $25

The red cross logo was on the boxes of both the single dolls and the gift sets. Since the boxes were also already in production, Mattel had to do something about the cross showing. Some one had the clever idea to design and apply a sticker that would cover the cross. The sticker reads "authentic uniform".

Army Gift Set White
#5626 • 1992 • $65

Each of the dolls came with chipboard cutout binoculars and dog tags. This was a bummer. I have substituted plastic binoculars I had around. I felt it made for a better display. As for the dog tags, I wonder how much more it could have cost to have had them made in metal? I'll ask Joe.

Army Gift Set Black
#5627 • 1992 • $50

Barbie and Ken dolls' uniforms are sand color camouflage outfits which would help them hide in the sand. The outfits are made of windbreaker fabric to shield them from the winds that would sweep across the desert plains. These dolls are another fine example of Mattel workmanship.

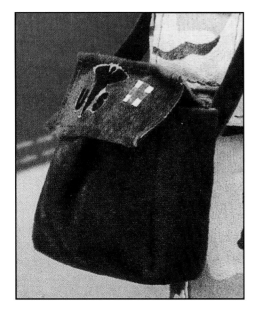

Army Gift Sets

Notice the red cross has been covered with a sticker.

Air Force Barbie White
#11552 • 1993 • $30

Mattel came back with another Air Force doll. This time Barbie doll is a Lieutenant Colonel; and is the leader of the Thunderbirds. She has trained well to lead her team of skilled jet pilots through daredevil maneuvers at an air show. 1-leader on the flight bag indicates Barbie doll is piloting the #1 aircraft.

Air Force Ken White
#11554 • 1993 • $30

As Captain, Ken doll is Barbie doll's 2nd Left Wing. Together they will fly in the Air Force's famous diamond formation. Often Ken doll's clothes appear a bit sloppy in fit. You can see here that these uniforms are cut and sewn to fit. Mattel really did a fabulous job, didn't they?

Air Force Barbie Black
#11553 • 1993 • $25

Barbie doll's makeup is perfect with her uniform. The red lips accent the jumpsuit, a hint of blue eyeshadow high lights the Thunderbird crest on the collar, and her soft ebony skin makes this doll the most striking in the collection.

Air Force Ken Black
#11555 • 1993 • $25

Black Barbie and Ken dolls have all the same rank and accessories as the white dolls. Each doll comes with a flight bag, sunglasses, hats, shoes, duffel bags, child-size badges, and hair brush for the dolls (not that Ken needs a hair brush).

Air Force Gift Set White

#11581 • 1993 • $60

One of the things that is interesting about gift sets is that Mattel seems to wait to release them long after the single dolls have hit the store shelves. This causes resistance in buying them, because collectors have already spent their money on the single dolls. Many people feel it unnecessary to buy them twice.

Air Force Gift Set Black

#11582 • 1993 • $50

This was the last of the series. All these dolls were available on every military base nation wide. They have been retired for many years and their prices are just now starting to increase. If you like them, now might be a good time to pick them up.

Summit Barbie White
#7027 • 1990 • $35

Collectors often forget that Barbie doll is for children too. Mattel, however, never ever loses sight of that. In 1990 Mattel put together a series of dolls called the Summit Barbie dolls. This special edition was to celebrate the first annual Barbie Summit. The Summit Series was available through regular line accounts as well as the specialty stores.

Designed by: Janet Goldblatt

Summit Barbie Black
#7028 • 1990 • $30

Mattel would set aside 50 cents for every doll sold. Mattel stated on the box that no portion of the purchase price of the dolls was tax deductible. These funds would be given to non-profit organizations that would assist children with education and literacy world-wide.

Designed by: Janet Goldblatt

Summit Barbie Hispanic
#7029 • 1990 • $40

Mattel would bring children from 30 countries together for a cultural exchange in which they would discuss hunger, freedom, ecology, and peace in hopes of making a difference. The children's input would be presented to world leaders.

Designed by: Janet Goldblatt

Summit Barbie Asian
#N/A • 1990 • $40

Another 50 cents from the sale of each of these Summit dolls would be set aside for future Barbie Summit meetings. Mattel's headquarters, at that time, were still in Hawthorne, California and you could have written them for further information. Often Mattel has some special offer on the boxes and I seldom take advantage of that. Watch for those kinds of things and participate. I am so excited about getting my dolls that I overlook the promotions. Later I wished I had taken advantage of them.

Designed by: Janet Goldblatt

UNICEF *Barbie White*
01920 • 1989 • $30

At the time the UNICEF dolls were produced, UNICEF was over 40 years old. UNICEF stands for the United Nations Children's Fund. UNICEF's primary interest is the needs of the children of the world. The organization supplies food, medicine, and clean water to less fortunate children everywhere.

Designed by: Janet Goldblatt

UNICEF *Barbie Black*
#4770 • 1989 • $30

For every UNICEF doll Mattel sold, 37 cents went to the United States Committee for UNICEF. This money would be used by the organization to help with projects around the world, as was true with the Summit dolls, Mattel stated that no portion of the purchase price of these dolls were tax deductible.

Designed by: Janet Goldblatt

UNICEF *Barbie Hispanic*
#4782 • 1989 • $40

Each box was clearly marked Special Edition and included a Barbie doll, formal gown, sash, jewelry, long gauntlets, shoes, doll stand, and a wonderful poster of the dolls called "The Rights of The Child". The UNICEF dolls were issued to both regular line stores and specialty shops, as were the Summit dolls. Box would have shown Hispanic doll.

Designed by: Janet Goldblatt

UNICEF *Barbie Asian*
#4774 • 1989 • $40

My UNICEF dolls are on display with my Barbie For President dolls and Blue Rhapsody. To learn more about these dolls see page 36, *Barbie Exclusives Book II,* and page 72, *Barbie Exclusives Book I.* Their royal blue chiffon gowns trimmed with red make a wonderful full display together. Try it yourself and see what you think. Box whould have shown Asian doll.

Designed by: Janet Goldblatt

Trading Cards
#5533 • 1990 • $100

It's nice to have something to collect that is just for fun and won't send us all to the poor house. Mattel came up with just that. They offered trading cards for collectors of all ages and all budgets. You could buy Barbie trading cards in several different ways: in packs of 10, or a 300 piece set, or the deluxe version, which was available only at specialty stores, as you see here. The set came with extra cards that you couldn't get any other way and with a vinyl binder that had the same print as the Barbie Style doll, which was an exclusive for the Applause Toy Company. Mattel also offered a poster that showed the trading cards. These were fun to collect, trade and to share and it wasn't expensive.

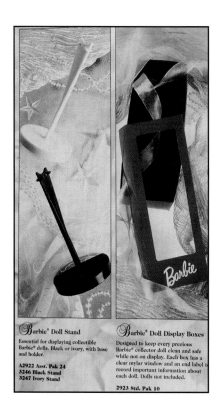

Stands
#A2922 • N/A • $10

Most of the collector dolls come with their own stands. Usually a stand inserts into a disc. These are saddle stands which go between the doll's legs and she rests on the saddle of the stand. Mattel offers these separately in either pearl white or black. They have been available for several years.

Boxes
#2923 • N/A • $16

Mattel offers Barbie-pink window boxes. They have multiple uses. These are wonderful for storing loose dolls, keeping them neat and dust free. They are great for gift giving too. I often use them to store odds and ends. The ends of the boxes are white and have lines so you can label the contents. It has been reported that the purple liner can bleed on to the dolls or clothing. I never had a problem because the moment I heard this I came up with a simple solution for myself; I merely put the liner in upside down. Others have chosen to put white tissue paper in the box. Either way, it's better to be safe than sorry.

Case
N/A• $65

For one season only, Mattel offered Lucite™ doll cases like the ones they used for the Gold Bob Mackie doll. They must have realized the future Mackie designs were not going to fit into these specially designed single-doll showcases. Bob Mackie's name was removed from the box and marketed separately. Once they were sold out, Mattel saw no reason to continue production. Photograph not available. See Mackie Gold, page 25.

ACCESSORIES

Catalog
N/A • $25

Collectors claimed they wanted catalogs. So, in 1991 Mattel had them painted. But collectors would not pay the $25.00 it cost. They didn't sell well and Mattel saw no reason to do it again.

Shoes
#10612 • 1993 • $5

Collectors are always screaming for shoes! One day I had a brainstorm. I thought that if enough voices were heard in force that maybe, just maybe, Mattel might respond. I took out classified ads in several trade magazines and solicited persons interested in buying Barbie doll shoes from Mattel. I sent petitions to all those who responded and handed some out at doll shows. The response was unbelievable! I sent all petitions to the desk of the Mattel president herself. A few days later I got a phone call from a gal at Mattel who asked me what everyone wanted. I told her open toe pumps (like those on the porcelain dolls), American Girl shoes, and t-straps. I knew I was talking to someone a lot younger than myself when the response I got was, "What's a t-strap?" Mattel supplied us with open toe mules. Thank you Mattel, now how about some more?

123

Equestrian Gift Set
Horse Only
#4045 • 1991 • $75

There were several horses sold in the United States in 1991. Champion was the only horse gift set sold in the specialty shops in America and in the foreign market. This special offer through the Timeless Creations division was unique in that it came with a separate equestrian outfit for the Barbie doll. You had to provide your own doll. I have selected Pretty Hearts Barbie doll, which was produced the same year, to model the outfit for you. The Champion horse and outfit you see here is from the collection of Bob Gardner.

Friendship Barbie
#3677 • 1991 • $35

There are a number of Friendship Barbie dolls for the European market only. Here is the only one that was available in the U.S. at specialty doll stores. The doll was part of a series of Friendship dolls done in commemoration of the tearing down of the Berlin Wall.

Benetton Barbie
#4873 • 1991 • $40

There were a series of dolls available that were produced for the foreign market only. Mattel allowed the specialty stores in the U.S. to carry the Benetton Barbie doll. Benetton is a foreign-based clothing company. They make really great high quality sportswear, often using brilliant bold colors at moderate prices. The value shows on all the Benetton dolls.

Designed by: Kitty Black Perkins

Sea Holiday Barbie
#5471 • 1992 • $40

Sea Holiday Barbie doll was available in the U.S. only at specialty doll shops, as were the Naf Naf and Benetton shopping dolls. Midge and Ken Naf Naf dolls were available in the international markets, import specialty stores, or at doll shows. The first releases of this doll had a camera inside the package with lipstick hidden in the lens. Later releases did not include the lipstick.

Designed by: Cynthia Young

Sea Holiday Ken
#5474 • 1992 • $40

A number of years earlier, Mattel experimented with a new male face mold. Sea Holiday Ken doll was made from one of the new molds. You might recognize this doll as Alan. This was one of the best male faces that Mattel has ever done. As Captain of the ship, he's looking pretty sharp! Both Barbie and Midge could go overboard for him!

Designed by: Cynthia Young

Sea Holiday Midge
#5476 • 1992 • $40

It is very funny that Ken, formerly Alan doll, is on board this ship. For awhile the joke was that Alan was posing as Ken to lure Barbie out to sea and dump her overboard so that Midge could have her wardrobe. All the dolls in this grouping have snappy nautical attire. The ship featured on the back of the boxes was originally for Europe only. The boat was very expensive and Mattel had some left over, which were eventually sold through FAO Schwarz.

Designed by: Cynthia Young

Party Changes
#2545 • 1992 • $45

Party Changes Barbie doll was so named, because of the versatility of her outfit. The chiffon petal skirt can be removed and used as a shawl, or attached to the bottom of the deep rose colored skirt, or wrapped around her waist. This allowed Barbie doll to have four completely different looks. This doll was available at specialty doll stores or in several foreign countries.

International Private Collection
#10772 • 1993 • $45

These fashions were designed and released for the foreign market. They were also available in specialty stores across the U.S. It is always nice to have something special or different for Barbie doll to wear. The opening price on these gowns was very affordable.

Crystal Carriage
#10142 • 1994 • $75

This horse and carriage was available to specialty stores, through the Timeless Creations Division and in the foreign markets only. That same year, Crystal Barbie and Ken dolls were available as regular line dolls in the U.S. and in several foreign countries and were sold as a gift set through the wholesale clubs. For additional information, see *Barbie Exclusives Book I*, page 134.

NAF NAF Barbie
#10997 • 1993 • $35

Naf Naf Barbie doll is one of the cutest sportswear dolls Mattel has offered to the specialty stores. Naf Naf is a European clothing company. Barbie doll was the only one that was available in the United States. Midge and Ken were available in the foreign markets.

Designed by: Kitty Black Perkins

Oshogatsu #1, Happy New Year
#14024 • 1995 • $175

Originally this doll was for the Japanese market and the U.S. specialty stores only. Things don't always go the way they are planned. There are three different box versions. The first shipments to doll shops had no Japanese writing on the outside, so Mattel quickly designed stickers with Japanese characters that say "Happy New Year" — a temporary measure until embossed boxes could be produced. The first releases had Barbie doll's shoes up inside the liner. The second and third releases have a slit in the liner; the shoes are wrapped in plastic bags which are threaded through the slit. O.G. as she has come to be referred to, is one of my favorites.

Oshogatsu #2, Happy New Year
#16093 • 1996 • $110

This second edition Oshogatsu Barbie doll wears an authentic Japanese kimono. The salmon colored dress is adorned with golden cherry blossoms, a Japanese classic design. Barbie doll's dark hair is a typical Japanese style with chin-length strands and straight bangs. Oriental themes have always sold very well. I predict that this OG 2 will be no exception.

Photograph courtesy of Mattel, Inc.

Andalucia
#15758 • 1996 • $35

Andalucia Barbie doll was created for Spain and Portugal and was shared with the United States at specialty stores. Before the doll was released there were some who thought she was the follow-up to Fantastica and Festiva. Although, Andalucia is not part of that series, the doll certainly displays well with the other two. The lush black hair is especially wonderful with her rich brown eyes. This Hispanic theme has been very popular with collectors. The gowns on all three dolls are particularly well made. Andalucia Barbie doll's traditional dress is from Andalucia which is a region in southern Spain that borders on the Atlantic, the Strait of Gibraltar, and the Mediterranean. All of these qualities make this doll a wonderful value.

Designed by: Golald Deen

Crystal Rhapsody
#1553 • 1992 • $500

Barbie doll's gown is of black rayon velvet and silk charmeuse which is delicately crystal pleated, hence her name. It is one of the most dramatically dressed porcelains to date. Barbie doll could not ask for a more elegant sophisticated look. This doll was also offered as a limited edition in brunette at the Disney Doll and Bear Convention. Crystal Rhapsody was the first in a series known as The Presidential Porcelain Barbie Doll Collection.

Designed by: Cynthia Young

Royal Splendor
#10950 • 1993 • $375

Second in the Presidential series is Royal Splendor Barbie doll. The China white skin tone is quite a contrast to the deep rich royal purple satin of her gown. Janet Goldblatt selected wonderful jewel-tone embroidery work to emphasize Barbie doll's splendor.

Designed by: Janet Goldblatt

Gold Sensation
A.K.A. Venus de Milo
#10246 • 1993 • $400

I could be cute and tell you that this is a one-of-kind Venus de Milo Barbie doll. But, that wouldn't be true. I prefer to call it the best of my before and after examples. The close-up was taken just moments before I dropped her. I don't advise dropping your porcelain dolls. The break was a nice clean break and my husband was going to glue it back together for me so you wouldn't have to see her this way. I decided it didn't matter; it gives me something to talk about, and I bet I'm not the only one to drop a porcelain doll.

Designed by: Janet Goldblatt

Silver Sensation
#N/A • N/A • $450

This doll was the second of only two dolls in the series. Silver Sensation seems to be a little harder to find than her predecessor dressed in gold.

Designed by: Janet Goldblatt

From the collection of Bob Gardner.

Star Lily Bride
#12953 • 1994 • $220

Brides are a favorite with most collectors. Star Lily Bride Porcelain is no exception. This is the first wedding gown for a series of brides Mattel has on the agenda. It will be interesting to watch the future to see if non-Barbie doll collectors, whose main interest is bride dolls will be seeking Star Lily. I know it is hard to believe that some people out there still don't collect Barbie dolls, but it is true that not everyone does. I wonder what it would be like to not collect Barbie dolls. Hmm?

Designed by: Ann Bray

Romantic Rose Bride
#14541 • 1995 • $200

This is the second in a series of porcelain brides for Mattel. Barbie doll is ready for the big day in her simple, but elegant wedding gown. The bouquet is not to scale, but does not detract from the doll's beauty; in fact it emphasizes it. The roses are so rich in color that they will draw your eye to this doll when she is on display with other brides.

Designed by: Damaris Vidal

Holiday Jewel
#14311 • 1995 • $225

For the first time Mattel offered the collector a porcelain holiday doll. It is interesting that they chose the colors that they did for the box. Teal green and orange has never been associated with Christmas. In spite of this break from tradition, the packaging is very dramatic. The actual doll was photographed with a softening filter giving her an angelic look. Barbie doll's dress, on the other hand, is very Christmasy. The green lamé sleeves and bodice with a blue and gold appliqué on top of the cranberry velvet skirt are very festive. This is the first porcelain doll with green eyes. The date on the box says 1995, but the doll was not released into the market place until 1996.

Designed by: Janet Goldblatt

Snow Princess
#11875 • 1994 • $125

Snow Princess Barbie doll was the first in a series of dolls based on, no, not that famous New York City restaurant, but the seasons of the year. This winter theme doll with her sequins and marabou trim is as white as the snow she was named after. This doll is especially decorative at holiday time.

Designed by: Janet Goldblatt

Spring Bouquet
#12989 • 1994 • $150

Spring Bouquet Barbie doll (could just as easily have been named June) is busting out all over. The spring floral bouquet is inspiration to run out and plant a garden. The pastel tones on the airy gown starts the season off well. Spring Bouquet's bonnet is one of the nicest hats Barbie doll owns. I wouldn't mind one like that myself. The name Spring Bouquet was also used on an exclusive in 1992. The dolls and the prices are extremely different.

Designed by: Janet Goldblatt

Autumn Glory
#15204 • 1995 • $100

What an appropriate name. Barbie doll does look as if she is in her glory, doesn't she? The fall colors continue the season theme well. It is the least elaborate and the most elegant of the series. Many of Janet Goldblatt's dolls have the most spectacular hats. She is a winner!

Designed by: Janet Goldblatt

Portrait in Taffeta
#15528 • 1996 • $175

When is the last time you saw Barbie doll dressed in brown? My memory on that goes back to the mid '60s. From her head to her toes, this doll is elegant. The feathered eyelashes emphasize her olive brown eyes. Taffeta has a great deal of sizing in it, which makes it difficult to work with. Mr. Best has done a wonderful job of softening it with gold lamé and plush velvet. Barbie doll's crystal earrings and rhinestone collar adds to her simple elegance. This couture doll cannot be well appreciated in her box. The early releases of this doll came with a plain cardboard-color liner and the doll is secured in her box with cardboard panels. In later issues the liner was changed to a plain white background. Box collectors were not overly happy with either model because you can not get the full beauty of the doll with all that stuff holding her in place. The box itself is wonderfully rich with the copper-colored lettering. You will want to handle this box carefully as the cardboard is thin and could damage easily. *Portrait in Taffeta* would be an asset to anyone's collection.

Designed by: Robert Best

Coca Cola
#15762 • 1996 • $150

This has got to be my favorite of the direct marketed dolls. It's fashion history in the present. This doll is the first in a series that I, for one, do not want to wait for. Unfortunately, we will have to. The series will have Barbie doll dressed in period pieces as were used in Coke advertising. The red and white dot dress with lace trim and rose adorned fedora could just as easily have been a valentine doll. If you are one who doesn't like buying your dolls sight unseen, watch for her at your specialty shop or doll shows. If you don't already own her, I think once you see her you will probably want to.

Angel Lights
#10610 • 1993 • $125

Angel Lights Barbie doll is not a doll at all. She is the first and only tree-topper for Mattel. She was offered at specialty stores. Many collectors did not want to put her on their tree because they were afraid that sap would ruin her gown. So many Angel Lights helped decorate the season on mantel pieces and tables, rather than on trees. No matter where you put her, she illuminates wonderfully and brightens any holiday home.

Designed by: Janet Goldblatt

Peppermint Princess
#13598 • 1994 • $150

Peppermint Princess Barbie doll was one of two holiday themed dolls designed by Geralyn Nelson. The other was a sister-piece that was only released in foreign markets. It is easy to see how Peppermint got her name with her billowing red and white skirt. The pattern that Geralyn used for this doll was utilized on the prototype for Winter Princess and was later re-designed. The same basic design would ultimately be used for Avon's first Christmas doll. Peppermint's bodice is luscious cranberry with matching drawstring evening bag. The skirt is white satin with several rows of red ribbon. Her gauntlets, faux-trimmed collar and matching hat accent the winter princess theme nicely. I sure miss Geralyn Nelson's designs. She made a lot of fabulous dolls for Mattel.

Designed by: Geralyn Nelson

Jewel Princess
#15826 • 1996 • $75

Jewel Princess Barbie doll for 1996 was specialty store only. This is fourth in the series which has become known as the Winter Princess Series. The first two dolls in this series were shared exclusives with the Home Shopping Network and specialty stores. To learn more about those two dolls, see *Barbie Exclusives Book II*, pages 45 and 46. They all have a wonderful winter theme and make colorful decorations at Christmas. Jewel Princess shares her trimmings with other dolls. Her buttons are the same as used on Peppermint Princess's earrings and for several other dolls. Her red jacket and plaid taffeta skirt are very festive. This doll is on loan from Bob Gardner's collection. Thank you, Bob.

Designed by: Ann Driskill

1988 Happy Holidays
#1703 • 1988 • $900
Red Gown

The 1988 Happy Holidays doll was a new and exciting doll for Mattel to end the year with. She was the finale for the year and the beginning of a new breed of collectors. Every year since, Mattel produced a new doll that collectors impatiently wait for. This series is not from the Timeless division, but rather regular line dolls. I decided to show them to you because so many collectors requested them. I won't be saying anything about them. They speak for themselves.

Designed by: Kitty Perkins Black

1989 Happy Holidays
#3523 • 1989 • $300
White Gown
Designed by: Kitty Black Perkins

1990 Happy Holidays White
#4098 • 1990 • $250
Fuschia Gown
Designed by: Kitty Black Perkins

1990 Happy Holidays Black
#4543 • 1990 • $125
Fuschia Gown
Designed by: Kitty Black Perkins

1991 Happy Holidays White

#4098 • 1991 • $250

Green Velvet Gown

Designed by: Cynthia Young

1991 Happy Holidays Black

#2696 • 1991 • $125

Green Velvet Gown

Designed by: Cynthia Young

1992 Happy Holidays White
#1429 • 1992 • $175
Silver Gown
Designed by: Cynthia Young

1992 Happy Holidays Black
#2396 • 1992 • $95
Silver Gown
Designed by: Cynthia Young

1993 Happy Holidays White
#10824 • 1993 • $150
Red Gown
Designed by: Abbe Littleton & Carol Spence

1993 Happy Holidays Black
#10911 • 1993 • $95
Red Gown
Designed by: Abbe Littleton & Carol Spencer

1994 Happy Holidays White
#12155 • 1994 • $175
Gold Gown
Designed by: Janet Goldblatt

1994 Happy Holidays Black
#12156 • 1994 • $175
Gold Gown
Designed by: Janet Goldblatt

1995 Happy Holidays White
#14123 • 1995 • $75
Green & Silver Gown
Designed by: Kitty Perkins Black

1995 Happy Holidays Black
#14124 • 1995 • $65
Green And Silver Gown
Designed by: Kitty Perkins Black

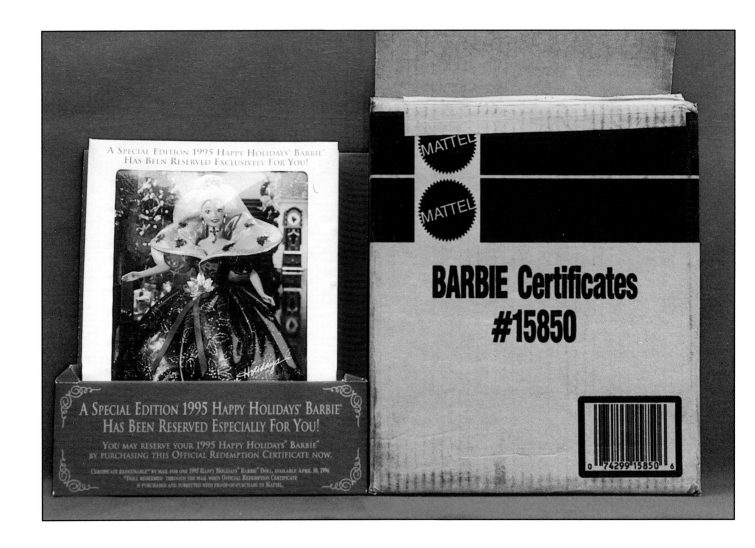

Voucher
#101695 • 1995 • $40

In 1995, the demand for the Happy Holidays doll was great and supply was very limited. To appease the collector, Mattel issued a pre-payable paper voucher which was distributed to accounts all across the country. After the sale, the buyer would redeem the voucher through Mattel, not at the store they purchased it from, an action which left many storeowners displeased.

Designed by: The marketing department I suppose.

1996 Happy Holidays White

#15646 • 1996 • $65

Burgundy Gown

Designed by: Ann Driskill

1996 Happy Holidays Black

#15647 • 1996 • $55

Burgundy Gown

Designed by: Ann Driskill

Photograph courtesy of Mattel, Inc.

Pink Splendor
#16091 • 1996 • $900

Pink Splendor Barbie doll has one problem and one problem only; not every collector can afford to own her. The opening price was extremely high. Many collectors became bitter. I have to admit that I was bitter too. Mattel includes surveys in many of their collector doll's boxes and they poll collectors at conventions, doll shows, and trade shows. The information that collectors submit is taken very seriously by the analysts. I believe that Mattel would not have produced this special doll if the statistics had not indicated a desire for something so amazingly different and expensive that there would be a market for her. There is a market for her. This doll is wonderfully constructed. The fabric is superb. Be kind when judging this doll; it's not her fault she is so expensive.

Designed by: Cynthia Young